THAT BLUE REPAIR

THAT BLUE REPAIR

To Spencer:
One of the true poets —
Blessings,

Joan

Joan Hutton Landis

Jan. 23, '09
Media, Pa.

PENSTROKE PRESS
Rochester, Vermont

PENSTROKE PRESS
145 Bethel Mountain Road
P.O. Box 119
Rochester, Vermont 05767

Text design by Ann Aspell.

Library of Congress Cataloging-in-Publication Data

Landis, Joan Hutton, 1930–

   That blue repair / by Joan Hutton Landis.
     p. cm.
  ISBN 0-9669177-5-8 (pbk : alk. paper)
  I. Title.
  PS3612.A54835T47 2008
  811'.6--dc22

                       2008025120

FIRST EDITION

This book is dedicated to Margaret Foster Hutton (1902–1984)
who gave me words

and to Kendall,
who made them imperative

CONTENTS

FOREWORD

"I AM TRAINING MYSELF IN THE ART OF RECALL": so begins one of several poems in a volume that goes often into the past to discover the shape and meaning of a life. Joan Landis regards the past much as she regards everything else, with candor and a fierce determination to see without apology or bitterness. Often, she finds the way to the past is obstructed, the perspective unreliable, the probable facts unwanted, the desire to deny or revise almost irresistible. Yet she persists, keeps her eyes open, acknowledges shame or disgust while pressing on with the insistent business of getting to the bottom of her experience.

The compulsion to see, measure, grasp, forgive, punish and savor is palpable on every page of Joan Landis's book. Her poetry is restless and without any trace of complacency. The life she charts seems to have been lived within the boundaries of the usual, the permitted. But within the authorized spaces opened up by these poems runs a relentless undercurrent of misgiving. Even where the narrative impulse dominates and the story told unfolds with a kind of steady, unsurprising purpose, there are jolts of language, wayward particulars, not-quite-mastered observations to complicate what would otherwise seem mere colorful anecdote. Some poets are content to evoke a characteristic episode or posture, but Landis will not rely simply on the flux of action the poem is made to convey. She is alert, always, to the potential significance inscribed in each object or gesture she summons. In her hands, the past betrays meanings that are other than the sum total of the facts she cites, and she never allows herself to seem quite content with the conclusions at which she arrives.

Landis's way of handling literariness is an aspect of the restless mastery that is everywhere apparent in her work. Drawn compulsively to echo and allusion, Landis betrays no slightest anxiety of influence. Her poems are filled with epigraphs and links that call to mind Bishop and Keats, Anne Carson and Wallace Stevens, Frost and Marianne Moore; she likes to get lost in the thickets of association, and likes as well to recoil, wondering where her own inclinations will lead. Attracted to sources and similarities, she is both thrilled and exasperated by the sense that everything has "its hidden twin," that nothing is merely what it is, original and unprecedented. Can a poet, head stuffed with favorite lines and images, nonetheless avow that she is "sick to death of all this poetry" she has taken in? Predictably divided, sassy and serious, passionate and unsentimental, Landis tackles her own literary propensities just as she engages her own commitments and defections as child, wife, mother and friend.

Perhaps the most startling manifestation of Joan Landis's literariness is her virtuosity with rhyme, a gift employed as a strategy for conferring unity and shape on the disparate material of which poems — and lives —are made. The persistent drive to rhyme, the search for the precise word or sound cluster that will suffice is an essential aspect of Landis's imagination. She takes in the accumulated data of the years and, without over-simplifying the content, comes to her own — often rhyming — resolutions. The rhymes seduce us with the promise of a unity that is, necessarily, ever gathering and unraveling. Rhyme patterns are briefly established and, as the poems unwind, disrupted, only to be confirmed, oddly, by newly emerging rhymes. Rhyme, for Landis, is itself a formal metaphor for the project of being-in-the world in which events seek their match, their meaning, through sound. The poems track her way to tentative, provisional harmonies through the discordant path of remembered experience. The process dramatizes, in ways that can be thrilling and unnerving, the poet's will to find, wherever she turns, an ever-elusive unity.

It is tempting, of course, to say of a poet as consistently good as Joan Landis that she sees as clearly as Bishop, feels as deeply as Frost, and demonstrates now and then the wit and humor of Phillip Larkin. But she is, in spite of the obvious echoes, doublings and allusions, altogether her own kind of poet. Is she a formalist? Say, rather that Landis is a poet who seems to think as she writes, whose thoughts take shape in the fits and starts of the language she invents as she goes. Is she a worldly poet? She is a poet whose knowledge of people and of sentiment seems always situated, so that the world that shapes her impressions always deeply matters. Is she a poet of elegy and retrospect? We learn, in reading the poems of Joan Landis, of losses endured and of the great weight of the past as it looms over present prospects. But there is, in the accent and fiber of Landis's writing, a stubborn will to be equal to everything that may come along that is relentlessly inspiring. This is not, finally, a poetry of regret or reserve but a poetry of cunning and instinct and of exuberant, virtuosic persistence.

PEG BOYERS
Executive Editor,
SALMAGUNDI

ACKNOWLEDGEMENTS

The author would like to thank the editors of the following journals where these poems first appeared.

Parnassus: Poetry in Review: Letter to Edward Taylor

The Gettysburg Review: Both

The Transatlantic Review: Morning Scene

The New York Times Book of Verse: Vain Dream for John Clare

The Gettysburg Review: Approaching Seventy, Parce que

The Far Point: On Having Misplaced a Favorite Book of Poems

Wesleyan Cardinal: Against Poetry

Philly Ink: The Tenth Anniversary Anthology: On Reading Ms. Bishop's
   Trouvée

Poetry: In a Bad Mood

The Far Point: The Sockdolager

Salmagundi: Lines for My Virtual Headstone, A Visit to My Mother's
   Grave, Rabbits (forthcoming)

Orchestra 2001: The Rainforest and Parce que, song cycle by Luis Prado,
   performed on February 23 and 25 in Swarthmore and Philadelphia

❧ I ❧

Sunday Lesson

Every Sunday at Kahdena, Grandfather would carve
a roast — beef, turkey, capon, lamb;
he was short because of the hump on his back
so stood on a box or stool to work.

I used to wonder how he could sleep,
always, perhaps, on one of his sides?
And why had my Grandmother married him?
Although he was kind and could quote from books,
he had another hump on his chest
that would poke her sharply if they kissed.

One Sunday I saw that the turkey he'd carve
had a bone in its breast that held up the skin.
It was pointy, a tent top or sideways kite,
exactly the shape of Grandfather's humps.
As he sharpened the knife and set to carve
I almost warned him not to cut.
Instead, I studied the rim of my plate,
its sheaves and shocks of white china wheat
which looked like the real ones on Kissel's farm.
Did every shape have its hidden twin,
breast bone and hump, pillar and shin?

Then Grace came in with the artichokes.
Her gray hair fell in skinny wisps
like the strings of old silk on Grandmother's shawl.
When my Mother put her hand on mine
and told me to eat before it got cold,
I saw that her hand was beautiful,
its tapered nails and smooth white skin,
but her emerald ring was an eye that cried
and under the knuckles, joints, veins,
the claw of the turkey hunched inside.

2

FISHER WEBBER

I am training myself in the art of recall
so try to remember my first four grades
at George Washington School in Morristown.

Kindergarten; it is 1934.
Ms. Bassett is young and kind.
Pictures of beans are pinned up on the wall,
string beans, green, with blossoms, bright red;
we sat in little wooden chairs
with seats that looked like a small behind.
I raise my hand to ask can I go —
oh, too late. The seat fills up.
I am sopping wet, ashamed. Ms. B.
leans down, whispers "never mind."

Was my first grade teacher Mrs. Towne?
Yes. Stern, dull, her brown hair ordinary.
I remember Eliot, a silly boy. One day
he threw up on his desk. It looked
and smelled like bad creamed corn. We heard
the vomit, stared — then turned away.
Later, I asked "Eliot, how do you feel?"
"With my hands," he replied, his eyes cold gray.
Like the motor of our black Chevrolet,
my kindness died. "You puked
and it really stank!" I said.
He turned from pasty white to splotchy red.

In second grade, we had Ms. Hart.
I see a round, flushed face.
Fisher Webber loved me, I could tell.
He offered me his sunflower pin.
"No thanks," I said. I already had one.
Martha-Jane loved him
but Fisher was intent on me.

His mother called mine on the phone
and asked if I could visit after school.
"Fisher's very sweet on Joan."
I said I'd go and wore the flowered dress
but when I saw his mother's car
waiting at the curb, Fisher in the back,
I said "No thanks. I can't today."
He hit the seat with his balled fist, turned
beet red. I walked away backwards
toward the safe, brick school.
Mrs. Webber sold shoes in a store.
Once she showed me the bones in my feet.
You could see if shoes fit in a flickering screen.
I remember her scarf, her anxious smile,
the bright red lipstick smeared on her teeth.

In third, the teacher was beautiful Ms. Day.
I dreamed of her at night
and thought about her round soft breasts
nestling underneath her sweater.
The day I left George Washington,
my father came to pick me up.
I knew from the look on his sly-fox face
that he, too, was imagining her breasts
and even how she looked, undressed.
I cried to leave my friends, those chalky boards,
my chart with gold stars, the small sun
somehow still flowering there,
but what could I do? We had moved.
"It's always the good ones who go," said Ms. Day.
I was sent to Alexander Hamilton.

Fisher Webber crashed a party that I gave
when we were all at Morristown High
in the unbearable ninth grade.
He brought a flask of whisky, drank it all,
unrolled our toilet paper down the hall,
poured baby powder on the living room floor,

mixed Halo and toothpaste in the sink.
My mother kindly stayed in her room
until they left, then burst out her door, furious.
We cleaned and mopped up the mess until one.
I begged her not to tell.
"Fisher Webber can go to hell," she said.
Then, "He never got over your heart-breaking snub."

Years later, in another town and state,
I ran into Sookie Spain, a classmate
from George Washington.
I asked for news of everyone, of Al
and Steve and Bobby G. and Martha-Jane,
of Ruthie Mace; and, finally, of Fisher. Her face fell.
One night, she said, going ninety miles an hour
in his mother's brand-new car,
Fisher hit a telephone pole, instantly killed.
I buried him deep in my memory.
Yet, on many nights in recent months,
his face beet-red, his fists balled,
he haunts my dreams —
sometimes a man, sometimes a boy,
still passionate; still unfulfilled.

The Rainforest

Cold settles in the shorn foot — as on the Russian steppes,
rain falls on the stumped space where the rainforest grew
and the birds, netted, egged on by habit, strain towards destinations
                now withheld;
even the thrusting rhubarb wilts, a melancholy beard.
            This frog has six legs.

Nothing is as it was in those poems
or those novels
that set up early expectations in Morristown, N.J.,
plots devoured in my green easy chair,
each plot a trusted land;
nothing — except the wordplay,
which finally will let you down,
which will betray you unexpectedly,
            like a husband.

Morning Scene

Horseradish anger
Like burnt buds
Tabascoes me from bed
I slam down stairs
Knives hang at the stove's spine
Fangs of steel
Glittery
Peels fall from the onion
In sheets of your skin
Gall
Is the mustard on the bread
My adrenalined
Cheeks roast
You'll pay
I burn your toast
Three boys skulk off to school
Your lips
Like two embarrassed frogs
Falter at my nape
Fool
I crack the shell
Of your bald skull
Crack
I rape the egg
How beautiful the yellow yolk
Dripping down the lucent cup
I breakfast on your brain
You smile
The sun stacks the back of pans
With grudging fire
Bright blurs
Damn the pain of pride
I slide my thrice-burnt hand
To yours
And tentative as embers
We go back up

LOVE POEM WITH GRACKLES

A man and a woman and a blackbird
Are one.

WALLACE STEVENS

Starlings and blackbirds
flock to fields and feeders,
then to poems
where they appear
as frequently
as blackberries.

Today, bigger, blacker
shapes fly in,
waves, invasions,
their iridescence like
an afterthought,
jewels undeserved.
All smaller birds take off.
It's clear —
that interposing of obsidian
that drinks the light
brings fear.

Not crows nor ravens,
they attack the seed,
each other,
beat their wings,
clean the chaff of suet
off their beaks, clack, clack,
go back for more —
pure greed.

My dog growls,
his hackles rise;

I whisper to him
"These are grackles."

Then your long shadow
tilts the room.
You look outside, say
"I see the Gracchi are back
from Rome."
The dog's tail wags.

I remember Cornelia,
her image in a childhood book,
one hand on each son's head.
Her gown is plain, unadorned.
"These are my jewels,"
the inscription said.

She turns these birds
to honored shades
flecked with opal,
onyx, jet;
I greet them, *salve* —
salvete — in Latin rusty
as a red-wing's song.

You sit, already deep
in some new book,
unaware of what transpires.
Amo, amas, amat, I say,
as if to memorize
this visit from
that lapidary city, Rome,
its bloody past,
your offhand wit
as convex glass,
heart's unexpected lurch
and rise.

I thank these blackbirds
flying off —
osculations in the dusk,
the Gracchi going grandly
home.

BOTH

In such clear winter Pennsylvania light
the view from this window is odd, skewed.
The bush in the foreground is ugly. It leans
to the right, its branchings like an x-ray of veins
gone wild with multiplying; or like whips.

Yet, the birds I love love it for some taste
inside its closed buds. Fennel? Artichoke?

The drive is a gray mix of gravel, grit,
the dull waste of cars. In this light
shadows change its shape, and if I strain
I see a modernist design, jagged, collage
unglued but ready to be beautiful. A Braque.

The rhododendrons and laurel and the lawn's edge,
still green in January, glitter. They are
hard, like certain women, rocking, rattling
in the wind. They say "beware, beware."

But in May, their garish blossoms will come out
and I will put them in the house in bowls
as countless women have, and moon and stare
at such rich flowering. Pistil, stamen, petal, stalk.

Suddenly, I think of Lucy walking in,
young and burnished with disheveled hair,
and though I am long-married, with three sons,
accustomed to the diamond in my ring,
know, if shame and old taboos
and fear of losing those I would not stun
had not, like lightning, x-ed my burning out
almost before it had begun
that I could love her with a passion wild as fire.

Or so I say, expecting now to know disgust
at both my selves, at ashen words like *wild* and *fire*.
The insight blooms, fades, too hard to tell.
I think about revision with a kind of lust,
revision of both image and desire.

The House in Goshen

The house in Goshen was one I adored.
Linc and sometimes Reggie lived in it
With my cousins, Becky and Ben. Linc had a cow
Who came up from the pasture when he called,
"Come Boss, come Boss." Soon she would calf.
We fed her roses when Linc was out.

At ten, we'd meet in the dining room,
Sit in spindle chairs, eat cheese, drink beer.
They'd let us each have one small glass.
They smoked their cigarettes, tap-tap
Lucky Strikes, Paul Jones, Chesterfield.
Off in the corner was the fenced-in well.
We looked down into its depths, heard echoes,
Saw our faces floating on the surface, calm.
But something rippled underneath
Dark, without a name, a scary thing.
Ben said it was an ancient child who drowned.

One summer, Aunt Reggie was "away," so we had
Myrtle Crumb to clean and cook. She was very fat.
She told us how her schoolmates chanted
"Myrtle P. Crumb, Myrtle P. Crumb,
Put a loaf of pumpernickel
Up her big bum." I didn't like her either.
She had crackly red hair and her thighs
Made a sucking sound when she walked.
She teased Ben who sometimes wet his bed.

One evening, she asked me to go for a walk.
Ben warned "Beware of the Boojums
If you go with Myrtle Crumb!
They hide in the bushes, jump out and strike
You dumb! Haha." But I went.
The familiar daisies glimmered in the dusk.

"How old are you?" she asked me, sly.
"Nine." "Oh, old enough. Know where babies come from?"
"Not from cabbages or storks!" was my reply.
"Promise not to squeal if I tell you how?"
"I never squeal," I said indignantly.
"Know how a man is hung, how he's slung?
What he looks like down there below the belt?"
I nodded, remembering Davy Rutan,
Taking out his withered little stump of flesh.
"Know how women got two holes?"
I wanted to turn and run back to the house
And look at the foxgloves that grew by the wall,
But told her, scowling, "Yes."
"Well, the man puts his thing in the woman's hole
and they wiggle and squirm until it feels good,
then he squirts some stuff called sperm up her tubes
and her eggs latch onto the gook from his pole
and that begins a baby."
I stopped walking and glared at Myrtle Crumb.
"No! My Mother would never do that!
She'd rather die and go to hell!"
But already I knew she was telling the truth.

.

The roadside daisies were white and pale,
The ferns moved too far to the left, then right.
"Now you got important news," said Myrtle Crumb,
her hand on her belly, tap-tap, tap-tap.

Back inside the quiet house, Linc reading,
Becky and Ben already in bed,
The harmonium stood in the sitting room,
The well was still in its shadowy place
But things all had a different look, sad, askew.
I got out my favorite paper dolls, Elizabeth and Margaret Rose.
They would never be told such disgusting news.
I changed their dresses and tightened the tabs.

Much later, back in Morristown, Linc told us
That Myrtle Crumb, no home,
No hope, no husband, no income,
Had suddenly dropped a pair of twins,
"So fat," he laughed, "you couldn't tell."
"Poor girl," said Mother, kind, not surprised.

Ashamed, I wished I could return
To the Goshen house before it was sold —
To the gardens, the cow, our cheese and beer,
To the terror we felt in the depths of the well
And warn Myrtle Crumb before she got lured
Out of her girlhood, into that hell.

CLOVER

The clover has been sipped
And scoured.
Bees hover over each pale flower
Searching for some secret savor —
Each a lover, hovering above
The other, trembling, a leaf.

My husband mows the clover
Down with his big mower.
The bees discover the slain blossoms —
I am filled with stupid grief.

The bees will sip at other flowers.
I recover, know, however,
Longing's power,
Love, like any flower —
                              brief.

LETTER TO EDWARD TAYLOR

Who in this Bowling Alley bowld the Sun?

EDWARD TAYLOR

I do meditate
Upon the sawdust fainting from the saw,
The vice, twice-collaring the wood.
Whom may I interrogate
If my vision of this
Be good?

I do laugh much
And mock contented things
To test if they be false
Or myself true;
I do dance much,
Asking in my turns
If I be pleasing to the waltz —
Of what pulse?

I do contemplate
The sugary source
Of things sweet,
Tasting the granular
Separation
And divorce of mold from thing
Baked
But know not
For whose sake.

I do cry
My whys in tears,
Yet make of salt no brine
Solution,
Disliking the pure pour
And spatter
Of dear water

If but effusions
Of no matter.

I do spin
In my small season,
Heartening the flax to definition;
I do feel
The shuttle start, the loom begin,
The fabric yearn
Toward fruition. By virtue
Of what reason?

I do love
What light refracts,
What bursts the nettings
Of my nets,
Skimming what butterflies
The summertime attracts
And then forgets.
What lets me?

I do discern
The falling and the lying down
Of doubt,
So praise, not knowing what to praise,
Until the skein of days,
Given,
Runs out.

❧ II ❧

Approaching Seventy

1. February

I like to ride backwards on the morning train
that takes me from my quiet book-bound house
toward the loud electric charge of Philadelphia.

I like to see the suburbs flying out,
bungalows all backing into pine,
still clouds in motion, the haste

of white saints flashing by in green backyards.
I smile each day at so much Catholic taste
in sweet reversal.

Suddenly, I find Anne Carson's perfect poem,
"Father's Old Blue Cardigan,"
stuck, upside down, a marker in my book.

I leave my backward seat, face front again;
think — I'll never lose my mind as Mr. Carson did.
Seventy is not so old. How old was he?

I name the station stops by heart — Media to Rye —
say, I'll never button up *my* heavy, woolen sweater,
acting out December in the transports of July.

2. March

Dawn
kisses open my half-resistant eyes,
its own *aubade.*
I think — morning light is an opal rug,
an invitation to new thickets.
Thickets? Rug? Christ! I turn over.

How many poems address the dawn?
I recite Anne Carson's spectacular lines:
"But as soon as the morning light hits my eyes, I want to be
out in it —
moving along the moor
into the first blue currents and cold navigation of everything
awake."
That gets me up.

Then, it's dull New England afternoon.
I walk the dog. He flushes a woodcock.
I try to remember the name in French — fail.
Nothing is anything but itself, except for the birches,
which look plagiarized.

I could once describe Persia or Timbuctu
so well you'd think you had just returned —
there might be sand on the floor, a smudge
of blue on the wall.
In April, I'll be seventy.
"Age cannot wither nor custom stale..." I begin to recite,
then stop. No new thickets, just old, learned lines,
the blind built by a life like mine.
Undoing his leash, I say to the dog,
"Such sad *Mercredis.*"
Is that my phrase or Ashbery's?

I'm turned around by an anecdote recalled:
Jeanette, half French, went to visit her mother,
one hundred years old, in a nursing home.
She'd been stalled in sad silence for days at a time,
wanting to die, not knowing how
but when asked what she had done that day,
touching a wisp of her thin, blued hair,
said to her daughter with nonchalance,
"Hier? Oh, hier j'ai dejeuné au Caire."
There is hope for the mind tomorrow —

it can go anywhere
                sailing on light
wild as a bird —
                bécasse.

Vain Dream for John Clare

Clare, John (1793-1864). The Northamtonshire
peasant poet. Wrote The Shepherd's Calendar
(1827), Rural Muse *(1835). Confined in a*
lunatic asylum.

THE READER'S ENCYCLOPEDIA

Oh, John Clare,
If only on some damp, dawn walk,
As you flustered frogs, froze misted quail,
Took happy care
To crush no kingcup, hedge no nesting hawk,
Delight in cranky caterpillar's trail —

You'd met me.
Stratagemmed with dew, I'd not have smiled,
But wreathing crowns of hawthorn, heightenend blush
To make you see
My eyes, my lips, my yellow hair blown wild,
As fairly as convolvulus or thrush.

I would, John Clare,
Have crazed with artifice your rustic passion
Until you loved me more than fern or mouse;
Then, when heart's despair
Was what you fought — frog fled, the blood-root ashen —
Have sheltered you, at least, from such a house.

Before "The Mousetrap"

Because of some great radiance I cannot name,
I fell in love with you when I was three.
Slipping free of Nurse's hand, I'd haunt the great hall
in hopes of finding you. My heart could scarcely breathe.
Once, you high-jumped out from some old tapestry,
Said "Boo!" to hoist me up upon your linen shoulders.
Looking down into your hair, I took a mouthful.
I taste it yet; salt, wheat, thyme, rue.
You called "Ophelia! Stop!"
My tongue and teeth, obedient, let go.
You were thirteen and golden as the morning bread.

When Laertes and my father said I should repel you,
I could not speak except in prompted lines,
nor eat. Such sadness has no saying.
I could not tell, how April last, compelled to meet,
we chose your father's orchard — full of snowdrops,
primrose, early violets, nor how our kisses, sweet
at first, grew until I thought I would go mad —
how you touched my cheeks, an elbow and my breasts —
until — before I swooned — I bit you.
You promised we would one day lie in your great, curtained bed
together; that we'd learn as one the two of bliss,
but not yet: only touch and taste and kiss and kiss — oh, Hamlet,
I am going mad. As you pretend to be.
I have gainsaid you.
And my father, I now see, is fool and hypocrite.
He sends Reynaldo off to spy in Paris on my brother.
He locks his bedroom door. The maid is in there too.
I hear him braying like an ass!
Oh, at his behest, I sent back all your precious letters.
I am like my father! Shame.

I will wait for you after the play tonight —
         more intolerable pain —
break the mold of custom —
         and disobedient for once,
         heart in my mouth —
explain.

First Sight

Allah Mubarak! It's going well,
guests in decorated tiers —
hot — we gave them little fans
(Hisham imports them from Japan)
no flies, first spray — then frankincense and myrrh.
Two red velvet chairs, Louis Quinze.
My Dima sits in one, gown white,
white veil, a lattice for her precious face.

It's four. I take his arm, lead him in,
Firaz — my second cousin's son, no
other wives at forty five,
substantial.
He sits down in his red chair, can't wait,
leans forward — quickly lifts her veil —
first sight.

She stares but does not move or blink.
I think of Ahmed at the gate, his charmed snake —
how, hunting in our cars at night
light stuns and blinds the young gazelle.
They stand. But then she turns, runs, throws herself
into my arms. *"La, Abi, la,"* she pleads, again,
again, as if she were a child. I hold her, pat her back,
"There, my sweetest heart," I say; she's shaking, wild.

The women sit — fans still, no ululation yet. They stare.
I know exactly what they think.
In just a year she'll bear his son, play cards, take sunset rides
in curtained cars, resent the second wife,
learn not to grit her teeth, ball her fists, resist.
I whisper in her studded ear — "There, my darling, there,"
and over her shoulder I look out at my guests
and wink.

AMHERST: JUNE 1873

for David S. Dodge, great grandson of Abby Bliss

Abby Bliss will call today
imperial — this note entreats
to bring me News of Syria —
Damascus — Saul — strait streets —

of Daniel's Sacred Empire,
new College in Beyrouth —
the sounds that Arab music makes,
ululation — flute —

Her gifts of the Exotic —
exchanged for cakes and tea
and other Sweet Particulars —
like flowers — thrust — at me

She once stood up at Holyoke
and gave her Soul to Christ
I sat — a Shylock — in their midst —
My Pagan parts — unsacrificed!

I will seek the Refuge
these Barricades afford —
to meet her now — as Foreign
as — Encounter with — Our Lord!

Emily! Come down — you're late!
Vinnie won't put out your cup.
Do not, dear Friend, procrastinate —
Or else — I'm coming up!

Her face — Determination —
Quick! — adjust my Crown
Comply — no Degradation —
this once — I will go down.

Amherst Noon

I've only known one woman
In all my looking life —
Who tells Monogamy as truth
Yet never is a wife —

I keep her, steady, singled out —
Wedding sound and sight —
To see her through an Amherst noon —
Darkness — dressed in Light

HOROSCOPE

Today, my horoscope said this:
Change, try gratitude, don't rhyme!
At once I threw my china pig to Jane,
(its coins showered out on the rug's blue ground)
the washwoman blanched at my wet kiss
and taking the long stairs two at time,
reeled — trying not to hear their refrain
footfall/pound, stress/sound,
contradicting astrology line after line.

I think of Shiki, or was it Basho —
promising his father to pass the big test
but unable to focus on history's facts
writing poems around the lamp's white shade,
on his sleeve, down the selvedge of his vest,
on the knobs of his knees and one big toe,
of stars and the laundering river's tracks —
stone thanking water, leaf turning to jade,
his horoscope stressed in each line made.

On Having Misplaced a Favorite Book of Poems

Here I am, Sir, dead of night alone;

I do not want the gentle corollary voices

of the willow or the water or the small field stone;

I do not want the way August rejoices

in the yielding of an aster or the facing of a poplar branch

to rain; nor the shuttle-sweet bee at the dome

of his hive; I want the strong, cantankerous clench

of your mind, Love, rank with summer, in a poem.

It

for Margaret Foster Hutton (1902-1984)

My mother had *it*.
She had it more than any other.
I recognized that quality at four.

My father had no *it*.
He yelled *shit* at mother
and at me; his other favorite was *whore*.

(Linda called me the *it*
girl once at Bennington,
not knowing what it meant.

I tried to make it fit,
wore it like a worked gown,
inviting assessment.)

Once, back at 99 Franklin Street,
on a cruelty jag,
he paraded up and down the hall

getting the dog to its feet
and me. We shouted at Mag.
Wagging and marching, we'd call

bad words at my mother.
Quietly, she closed her door.
But next morning she smiled,

beating eggs to a yellow lather,
mopping the mottled floor,
no accusations, no silenced child.

I can still taste the shame
worse than vomit in my mouth
and feel the weight of love

when she said my name,
Joan, uninflected, without
anger or disdain. She was above

stooping. That was a palpable *it*.
Then we moved, she and I, to Kahdena,
the house I adored,

where Grammie would sit,
drooling, rocking, gnarled, cleaned
and fed by starched Nurse Ward.

When the car door slammed
on the flesh of her upper arm,
my mother never winced, cried

out nor dropped the long-stemmed
flowers that she held, no tone of alarm
because, I think, I was inside.

She simply said to Mr. B.,
"Please open the back door."
The bruise was purple, yellow, green;

it hung on her arm for all to see,
a natural jewel that she wore
like a bracelet, or sign, to mean

it. When Reenie Ullmann cut my hair
all off, my mother stroked my bald head
and said she liked that style,

an *it* almost without compare.
I heard Aunt NoNo's voice; it said,
"Give Joan an inch, she'll take a mile."

When I was twelve, we went to Florida by train
to institute the "great divorce."
I stonewalled all the lawyers who

asked for proof that Lewis T. caused willful pain,
was brutal. I only loved the Morgan horse
I rode and Mother, both completely true

to rein and spur and to my sullen self.
I wonder if I thought about her pain
or how her quiet humor flourished even there

inspite of her new status, "on the shelf,"
checks that never came, torrential rain,
no friends, the war, my melodramas of despair.

Once, when I came home from boarding school,
she let me meet a man she didn't like, she said,
whose leer and bourbon breath left no doubt

what was going on. Did she take me for a fool?
I caught them, later, getting into bed.
I called her "whore," ordered him, "Get out!"

Then, on some vacation when I slept and slept
she begged me to get up. "It's after one o'clock!"
A scream — then the smash of wood and glass shatter-

ing. I found her on the porch roof. Busily, I swept
shards up; she climbed back across the sill, in shock.
"Don't worry," when I left, "nothing serious the matter."

I said she never stooped. Nor did she fall
except for moments in my rigid expect-
ation; I was jealous and tyrannical. She understood.

She's now long dead. Still, I "love her all."
I think of, talk to, thank her and inspect
remembrances which tell me how she could

withstand so many years of loss and strain.
Of course, that splintered sash
lurked, dark boundary, the craze of glass,

to warn that bruises, uncomplained
of for too long, could compel that sudden crash —
her failed jump. She said her only suitor was catas-

trophe. I hear Aunt NoNo's voice repeat
"Give Joan an inch, she'll take a mile."
Mother told me once she loved all latitude,

teaching me the wild way words were sweet
to say and sound, to savor and compile
in diaries and poems. Because of gratitude

for that I still aspire to definition
of my mother's *it*.
I try, then tear it out, like sad Penelope.

My mother gave me love; no limit, no condition.
I took it, small Narcissus, all. Unwritten
yet, the proper poem will not be elegy

but weave together lines finally befitting
Margaret; her magnitude, her quality.

Against Poetry

Not Ideas About the Thing But the Thing Itself

Wallace Stevens

I'm sick to death of all this poetry about the Caribbean
and those cerebral islands poets sun their figured bodies on!
Let's go there!
Let's rent a room with mean hibiscus on the porch.
Let the landlady have a wart on her nose
and the black boy, rum-agreeable, lose all the keys!
You'll talk to the locked door in French, muttering,
Alors and *Quoi donc*, and scorch it with your silliest contempt.
I shall watch you from the corner of my eye,
catching the way your heels run down, the jaunty misfit of your
      tie.
You shall not, then, be exempt from any of the habits
married life, its attitudes, have put on me and I shall court them,
      willfully,
and stare into the late champagne, forcing myriads of sullen
      bubbles there
but try to see them as a thousand sour bubbles, not
as constellations of despair. We both are tired of traveling.
You comb your hair. You whistle. You apparently prepare.
I shiver. Getting up, I too prepare.
 Just this once, I shall expect no trappings of romance;
you will be distracted by the plants in their tropical too-much,
you'll stick a blossom in my hair where it will lean, ridiculous,
a platitude, and wither there.
And I shall wish we hadn't come and you will touch my funny
      bone
and inadvertently, I'll laugh, longing to be at home again
with piles and piles of magazines for easy satisfaction.
I'll wish you drove a truck or had the whole of "Lycidas" by
      heart,
making, as always, of utter things, an art that's less than art,
dissatisfaction with reality.

Then, I will take comparison with awkward grace,
and metaphor and simile and irony and paradox —
all the old abstractions I have idolized and so displace them there
behind the drapes, terrible with patternings of peony
and butterflies and flowery shapes, and close them
on the other-singing sea and shut the Sirens from my ears of
        possibility
other than this moment and this place and taking in my two
        cool hands
your unfamiliar face, will know it as it is;
will kiss the outer edges of your lips and kiss them so the nothing
need be said, and kiss and answer kiss until the muscles pull
like aching muscles at my head and I shall so impose your lips
on mine that then we must discover both the kiss itself
and the dominion of the lover;
and still I'll kiss and kiss until that whole willed
fundamental bliss shall make of that strange latitude but this;
and we will know a Caribbean island for an ocean shelf
and love, not as some idea of love, but love itself.

❧ III ❧

ADDRESSES

We go backward and forward and
place there is none

ST. AUGUSTINE

Born on Maple at Dr. Mills' —
For two full weeks
my mother gazes out her window
into April, its maples.
She forgets her winter grief —
feels, now, as the trees must, joy
at such swelling, greening,
budding — then —
that bursting into leaf.

*

A house with a hedge in New Paltz, N.Y.
near rich Uncle Sam's. His house is bigger.
There, velvet drapes make day like night.
The parrot screams *Ella, Ella,* and the maid
runs out, fooled each time.
Uncle Sam has the Stewart red hair.
He pays me a quarter to scratch his head.
I hate it; the oil, the wavy feel; like my father's.
Daddy spanks me for running toward the hedge —
I wanted the chestnut shining there —
"Why?" asks Mother, crying too.
His hairbrush hand hits, hits.
"She was going to run into the road," he said.

*

Kahdena Kahdena. My Grandmother's house.
What does it mean? Nobody knows.
"A made-up word," says somebody tall.
Uncle Phil's ceiling, a deep blue ground,

has stars pasted on; then, at the turn
of the stair, a tall glass stains me in color.
I come down, a queen
in a long rainbow gown
and in the center of the lilac grove,
deep in the shadows, white and round,
is a birdbath made of shining stone;
over and over, it's there, to be found
at *Kahdena*.

*

At four I live on Franklin Street.
Daddy says the Swirskys are *kikes*.
I tell Jean. She sobs.
Her mother wrings her red hands and cries
"Morris! Morris!"
He turns white.
Why? What are *kikes?*
the word is like lightning — forked —
                    it strikes.

*

Three Conklin Avenue, Egbert Hill.
It used to be Morristown's model house.
Gardens terrace it; steps
ascend to it. On these, snakes doze.
My mother bravely breaks their backs.
She pities the snakes
but says they make Aunt NoNo scream
and the doctor walk into the primrose bed;
I call it *conking on Conklin;* she likes that.

When Carol Polhemus stays for lunch —
fat and plain —
we four crowd into the breakfast nook.
I see my father's shoulder dip, his arm

go under the tabletop; his hand
edge up between her legs. He rocks.
She sits stock-still — her mouth an o.
I take my knife, strike the plate;
it breaks. Nobody speaks.
Let's go. I pull her up — we run.
Will she tell? I don't know.
Did my mother see?
I sit up high in the dogwood tree —
its forked branch —
until it grows dark, vow
if he ever touches another friend
to kill him.
Next day, he staggers back
from wherever he goes,
moans *shit, oh shit.*
Meanwhile, I write. I learn that trick,
sometimes transcending the facts; the *it.*

*

A numbered street in Miami Shores.
It's 1942.
We board with Miss George
who burps and farts, half her stricken stomach
gone. We die of not laughing.
The lawyer asks if my father was mean.
Tell me, he wheedles, *tell me, Joan.*
I freeze on the edge of his black leather chair,
my stare, Medusa's, turns him to stone.
When I fall off the running board of Luther's sedan,
the mirror exposes my elbow bone.
The room swoons —
but I have Shamrock, a Morgan horse.
Only Luther and I can ride him well.
He canters me over sand and ledge in Florida,
a state at the bottom edge of the map.

He is my touchstone, my mythical horse —
I learn how love annuls divorce.

> *

West Road, Norfolk, Connecticut.
Mother moves up to help Uncle Linc
and care for my cousins, Becky and Ben,
because Aunt Reggie's gone crazy again.
She's locked up tight in the loony-bin
but sometimes escapes, comes back, like a ghost
nightgown wet, weeds in her hair,
scaring my cousins almost to death.

I think of her curled in the corner chair,
smoking, listening to Bach by the hour;
I chose her to be my godmother once
liking her most of all the aunts,
her sideways glance, her root-cellar breath.
She'd let the dishes pile up in the sink
and the vegetables rot in the kitchen bin.
I used to watch her dream and think.
None of us ever mentions her name,
not *Reggie, Mother, Aunt, my wife;*
cuckoo was thought but left unsaid
as if poor Reggie was already dead.
I dreamed she rose out of Toby Pond,
godchilded up from her *slough of despond.*

> *

Stoneleigh-Prospect Hill School,
Greenfield, Mass.
The arrogant sound I need
lies
          in the double name.

Names are clothes,
glamorous or plain.
The first night I tell them "My name
is Joan but my friends call me Dusty."
The perfect lie; they fall for it.
I invent a new stride,
half cowboy.
One Saturday I drink a half-pint of rum
to ease my cramps and — captain
of the soccer team — charge onto the field,
glasses taped to nose and brow —
I'd broken the parts that hook over the ears —
to beat our rival — Burnham. I hear loud cheers,
am so dizzy I nearly fall but see a ball,
kick it hard and make the scoring goal.
Hurrah for the glorious Corazons! *Go Dust!*
Mrs. E. can smell the rum
when she bestows her grateful kiss —
is too polite or smart to ask
or look at the blood leaking down one shin.
My picture's in the yearbook with a lop-sided grin.
My glasses confess that I am blind drunk.

*

Bennington College, Bennington, Vermont.
Battles recur in these pastoral greens,
Parnell versus Dante, Pope versus Blake;
we argue, revise, retreat, take
sides, then justify the enemy. Heaven!
New fathers appear.
Belitt, Kunitz, Fowlie, Burke,
Nemerov, Burkhardt, Aaron, Fromm;
we rise to defend our assaulted work
and fall to them nightly in Oedipal dream.
We know there are serious lines to cross;
map some, but admit we are still too green.
On the surface, all is funny or sex.

The monument wilts when the girls go,
one wag says. We love that.
Because we are virgins we cause what's erect.
We drink, neck, sow our wild oats,
Crazy Janes in strict scarlet coats.

       *

Mrs. Longfellow's flat between Park and Lex.
To study again with Stanley Kunitz
is to own a penthouse at the Ritz.
On weekends, my loneliness fits
me, white gown, to a T;
dustcovers shroud chairs, snood one settee,
I compose sad poems, contentedly.

       *

18 Cornelia Street.
You are born into my life
Everything shines
Of the hours and minutes and seconds
I say
        These are my jewels.

       *

Paris; sept Rue Git-le-Coeur —
We love each other again and again.
It shows.
As I swell they ask — *Quand? When?*
I laugh — to think I am a house,
sa tour,
how I embody those two French words,
amour
and *chatelaine.*

       *

The *Asifa* Building, Ras Beirut;
cock cries crack open the dawn at five,
huge cockroaches clatter across the floor;
one baby dinosaur lays her eggs in the dregs
of the sherry; they hatch, swim; even you shudder.
When Lucian gets drunk on our whiskey sours, walks
into the sea, we fish him out in his Brooks Brothers' suit,
pure comedy. An earthquake mutters,
cracks race across the cinema walls; we stay
on to watch *How to Marry a Millionaire.*
Wedad has run into the open field
with Christopher in her arms.
Why not you come back? She's enraged.
Zilzal, zilzal. Wildly, she packs.
Up in her village, twenty are killed
when their houses of stone collapse, crush,
bury them. We eat *mezze* in *Zahle,* hear the next day
that two hundred die of the goat cheese we missed.

You fight with Mike Arnold, call him *mejnoon;*
pissed off, he orders us back to New York.
I cry at such waste; it's too soon! *Harram!*
We book on the *Andrea Doria,* suite fifty one,
then leave a week early so don't get scooped up
on the Stockholm's prow; don't drown; spared.
We vow to go back to Beirut. We loved it.
We were lucky there. *Hazz, hazz.*

*

317 East 10th Street, New York City, New York.
We learn its various dimensions,
its windows, French, its southern light.
The ceilings measure fourteen feet high,
two marble mantels, 1883,
one small garden in the back
with weeds and a central apple tree.
You throw away two dentist's chairs

and twelve old pairs of false teeth molds.
We three move in.
One night you number
all my body parts,
feed me ten green grapes
then push one deep inside my womb.
We laugh until we cry,
Let's multiply, you say with wit;
I add, or *fructify.*
And we do,
on 317 East Tenth.

*

Kilo Five, the Mecca Road.
Jeddah, Saudi Arabia.
Through the scorched air perspective is odd.
At six, the sun is a burst stain.
We watch the pilgrims, draped in white.
They look like chickens packed in a crate,
being trucked out to the great, black stone.
From our distant porch we cluck
in pity and disdain. You quote the first lines
of *The Canterbury Tales.*
Then you get off the path:
I herd you back —
          animal pain—
I retaliate, I get off too.
We go haywire; strike, fall,
locked, a wild kneeling on the bedroom floor.
From amplified towers, *muezzins* call.
The children have circles under their eyes.
Dumb from so many weeks of strain,
we simmer down
and I know in my pilgrim's heart of hearts
that Canterbury will pertain.

*

It is impossible to fairly say
what Beirut was like from 1962 to 1967;
each night, each day — a mix;
sometimes like hell, at others, heaven.
We lived just off Rue Bliss,
the Malas Building, T'aalat al-American —
heard the trolley's dawn clang and clank —
saw men stand by the walls to piss;
in summer, the stones of the city stank.
But looking up at Mount Sannine,
its cap of snow, the aquamarine sea below —
some things that I hated, blurred —
teased hair with rhinestone roses nested in it,
those little songbirds,
ortelans — served at parties *en brochette* —
the flies that swarmed at beggar's eyes,
the trots, the soaking sweat.

Soon, as if under a spell, we fell
into some new mood; a kind of awe.
The stones of crusader castles told us
history as did the bold, red-headed,
freckled kids who played around the Krak.
The fossil fish we found in rocks at Hakel,
skeletons still clear and crisp as lace
after millions of years under the sea,
now surfacing high in these rock-faced hills —
were, as Christopher said — big thrills;
things shone, patined, like Roman glass.

Once, up in a summer house above Ainab,
our orange canary somehow escaped
from his lacy white Tunisian cage.
We could see him flit from pine to pine.
Then, Miriam, the Eddy's maid,
held up a cucumber slice — began to sing;
Yussef Effendi followed her back to his cage
and under Miriam's magical spell, went in.

*

It's 1966. Ruth gives us summery Pig-in-a-Poke
in Rochester, Vermont, that place — its name a joke —
we call *the farm*. I think of its primitive kerosene stove,
the outhouse, sweet, in the wild-grape grove,
that chokecherry tree where birds flock in the fall,
to get drunk on chokecherry alchohol —
of racoons, porcupines, silver fox,
the odd concretions, other found rocks
and indigenous stones that Ruth collected —
one of her hard passions. This is the place recollected
each time I fly. Safe ground; green heaven.
Ruth bought it for a song, sight unseen, in hungry 1937.

*

East St., Middletown, Connecticut.
Josh says, "We've all come west to land on East."
That cracks us up in our split-level ranch.
We call for our servants; Naji, Rose, George,
Blanche: they don't reply.
Suds and polishes foam at our touch,
pictures go up, the house shines.
All five of us go back to school.
There, poems fly to my hands like birds.
The sumptuous act of connecting words
leads me back to the lilac grove,
to Kahdena, its white, found stone.
I live in that numinous world for days,
then overhear Ethan tell Nicky Soames,
"She just sits and writes her stupid poems."
Finally, you read a few lines, ask what I meant.
You, too, are cross; estranged.
I smile on the purple, East St. couch,
hear myself, from a distance, say
          words, not you — my true Orient.

*

550 Elm, Swarthmore, Pa. 19081.
The box bushes block the pour of light
the hemlocks next to the house are ill,
scaled, off-white.
This address itself announces blight.
You fritter away at the edge of the yard,
infected too.
I turn to the past, the Renaissance;
find that Shakespeare writes what I already know,
his "nook-shotten isle of Albion,"
Hamlet, Leontes, Antonio.
Oh, I excel at his sadness. Love? "Fie, fie."
I am Desdemona, her green black Moor,
and Iago, their pornographer. But I refuse
to say, as Desdemona did, "Faith, half asleep."
"Light, I say, light!" now Brabantio.

Then, I decide to get over it.
I learn again the comic mode, the intricate
ways of those *problem plays,* Vienna, Troy.
I study Helen in *All's Well That Ends Well,*
her original fall, her pilgrimage to another place,
the longed-for heaven which embeds a hell,
that boy,
Helena's absolving art: forgiveness, grace,
or seeming grace.

I say, "Physician, cure thyself!"
And I do.
I get a doctorate,
I clean the house.

*

1726 Locust Street, Philadelphia, Pa. —
Rittenhouse Square — like St. Stephen's Green.
The Curtis hires me, sight unseen,

to teach musicians honeyed words, to play
"asides upon their oboes." Music pours
from all the windows and all the doors.
I think of Larkin's poem — "Trees"
those leaves that, each day, *thresh,*
afresh, afresh, afresh.
They play like angels. I walk on air
and every night — prepare — prepare.

Pamela Frank, Scott St.John,
Jonathan Biss, Hilary Hahn,
Leon McCawley, Richie Hawley,
Gloria Justen, Soovin Kim,
Jessica Thompson, Ignat Solhzenitsyn.
Yevgeniy Sharlat, Margo Tat,
Katerina Englichova, Hsin-yun Huang,
Eric Zivian, Quirijn deLang.
Robert Walters, Yumi Huang,
Jennifer Orchard, Burchard Tang.
David Horne, V. Beranger,
John B. Hedges and Sharon Wei.

Their very names make music —
it is the music of the spheres,
at least to my enchanted ears.

I sop it all up in this new place; we swap
Schumann, Schubert, Bruch, Bright Sheng,
for Chaucer, Donne, Dickinson,
Bronte, Bishop, Annie Proulx,
Carson, Heaney, Olds, Muldoon.
They breeze through stories, novels, plays
when it's convenient; soon
it's well-known that I am lenient —
some play me for a fool;
but when it comes to Shakespeare and to Joyce,
a few desert their cellos and their flutes;

they are seduced by Sirens, and the voice
of Hamlet, Dedalus and Bloom;
                    at last, we're in cahoots.

                *

We buy the house the day it is shown;
it looks and smells like Kahdena.
In the butler's pantry, we stroke
the burnished wood. No, you say,
you cannot paint the dark, stained chestnut in the living room
white or blue. You do admit we need more light.

I don't consider the name of the Lane —
Osage, in Media, Pa., until we've settled in.
Oh God! Another tree!
Sage means wise; is a fragrant herb,
but the hard, green inedible fruit
that falls from the trees beyond our hedge
is not a good omen.
I have heard that Lewis or Clark
brought the first one back from Oregon.
It is tough and hardy — that's a plus!
Our mailman says the wood is used
in building the hulls of boats. It is strong
and flexible. It is also found in bows
for archery. Others claim
that it is native to Arkansas and Texas
where it is grown and clipped for fence;
its long thorns keep the cows from wandering.
I hear them low at night.

The movers put my Cornish in the cellar,
too tired to hoist it up the stairs.
An extra pedal changes the piano's tone
into a harpsichord's. It belonged to my mother
who painted it white with trim of gold.
Once, Eric played it down there in the dark

and the whole hushed house
filled with Couperin and Bach.
You finally give it to the Y; a tax deduction.
I cry. Our bones thin.

I say to hell with addresses and what
they can portend. To hell with osage oranges,
the dead-end lane,
the house's creaky stairs and crumbling stucco;
daily rounds, approaching age.

One night, I'll read you all my poems,
tell you exactly what they mean
incase they fail to say;
nothing gnomic, nothing slant;
I'll forgive your giving of my Cornish
so high-handedly away.
Shall we plan a trip to Paris or Arabia?
No — let's go to some new place; no memories,
no habits or nostalgia there! No thorny fence.
no name of tree or plant!
I confess this wish
and you, so down-to-earth, remark
that probably until our deaths,
we can't.

*

I dream all winter of Vermont,
our house, its new blue door,
the door sill where I sit and write;
stone walls ungainly moose step over,
our rocky fields, the music of the coyotes
and the birds — those things I love,
you — out planting measured rows
of beans, kohlrabi, chard.

I keep imagination's wily eye
on days and nights in mid-July
when phosphorescent meadowsweet
lights up the dusk, the spider webs,
the milkweed and the upper field
where Margaret's unsown garden grows,
her unstrewn, boxed-in ashes lie.

This dream of place is where I hide.
Stone, rock, lilac, tree —
but incantations — used through time —
lose melody, lose power
to stem this growing fear and grief.
What should I do?
Think of the golden chanterelles,
the rich duff, its smell, in the woods
the white, frail, Indian pipe —
think of the light on our sun-struck pond,
the sight of our maples again in full leaf.

I yearn to travel to the north;
that green domain;
                    what lies beyond.

*

❧ IV ❧

FISHING

My husband took two of our grandsons
Out to the inlet of the pond to learn to fish;
Kyle and Ryan. I call them Kai and Rye.
One has the surprising Stewart hair, red,
The other, the more familiar family blond.

I think about how all our boys, now men,
Learned this skill when Edwin Harvey dug our pond,
The single summer when no fish would hatch,
The prize that Ethan won for landing ten.

After an hour, they come back, bragging of the catch,
The creel holds ferns and nine brown trout,
The kind that self-stock every year.
Where do they come from? Up the stream,
But no one here can quite explain
Fish generation; source and time, a mystery.

They spread the nine, some twitching, still alive,
On the wooden planks outside the porch.
My husband shows them how to hold and place the knife,
Cut off the head, slice then gut. Both boys watch,
Step back. Kai's kindness keeps him mute.
Rye asks about the orange clusters in some fish.
Those are eggs. It's called the roe. Rye turns away.
Can't you tell the females from the males?
No, my husband says, distractedly, not when fishing, why?
Because you're murdering their babies! he explodes.
How can you do it? It's not — just!

His father tried to say how natural it was to fish,
Done by man since time began,
That fish did not, or probably not, feel pain,
That many pregnant females still were in the pond.

But Rye could find no comfort there or understand;
He went and stood beyond the apple trees, alone.

I vowed to tell him adults rarely find a way
To talk about their own brutality, or see it;
That fishing was for some a real necessity
but he was right and brave to take the fishes' side.

Later on, we ate the nine brown trout,
Dipped in flour, browned in butter, gently fried.
Rye refused to taste them,
Ate potato, chard, some stale cornbread.
Somehow, my chance to tell him how I empathized,
Shared his deep disgust at hooking, killing fish,
Admired his choosing of the great word — "just,"
Darkened like the day, then guttered
And went out.

On Reading Miss Bishop's Trouvée

Miss Bishop asks what a white (and red) hen,
run over, was doing on West 4th Street.
She provides the poor hen a fitting end;
it stars, a smash-hit, in her off-Broadway poem.

But seriously, did she ever love and lose a cat
as great as my late, lost Granville?
He had one white spot in the middle of his back
which set off his tigerly gray and black stripes;
his name the eponymous name of our town.

He could leap with such amazing grace
you might think of the late great Nijinski;
I hated his hunting, the high-pitched squeals
of the mole or mouse, its agonized squirm,
the fact of the indigo bunting's
small blue body on the red porch rug.
My husband coldly quoted Keats:
T'is the robin — ravening the worm.

I used to take the chipmunks from
my cat's reluctant jaws, then free them;
I'd see them run on three legs towards some ferny
dell — or green hell, I suppose — who knows?

Granville would sleep on our big bed.
He liked to put his head next to mine
on the soft, goose-down pillow. Oh,
Sing willow, willow, willow.

He used to somersault down a slope,
then lie on his back and grin;
he'd come in, then go right out again,
when it rained, he'd sleep and sleep, then mope.

Granville is gone. Fisher? Catamount?
Heart attack? Revenge for our week-end away?
The chipmunks know it. Brazen, they play
With our birdseed, tomatoes, count
On our kindness – grief – disarray.

Do I wish that Ms. Bishop would come
with her pen and an elegy? Yes, but much more,
that Granville would come, high-jumping
in through the hole in the screen, pause,
a vole — even an oriole — in his feathery jaws,
its wing real, its small beak broken again.

Our rugs are no longer half askew.
They lie on the floor — flat and smug.

MRS. HARRIS THINKS ABOUT BUSINESS

Today I did my business with ease
at eight forty-six.
Painless, no straining, there were two,
Both firm, well-shaped.

I caught a glimpse of last night's
baby peas in one
and golden flecks of prune.

Nanny used to punish us
for doing something in our pants
or beds. She'd smack us
if we ever said *poopoo, kaka,
pewey, doots:* our cousins' words.
She even hated *number two.*
Business, she would insist
pointing, with disgust,
is the proper name for it.

Just once, I should have called
a spade a spade:
"You may call it business
but its proper name is shit."

That word still makes me blush.
What stupid sources for our shame!
It's hard to change.
I'll say *asses* now instead of *fannies*
I've *peed* instead of *leaked* or *wet.*
Could I call my feces nannies?
No. Someday, not yet.

To produce your business nicely
when you are ninety-three,
brings feelings of relief,

delight and secret pride;
I bless my bowel's fruitful work,
its gassy blurts, familiar smells.
Enjoy its commerce while you can,
its rich economy.

In a Bad Mood

The fish are jumping in the fucking pond,
Mike's pigs are fucking in their nasty sty;
I know you want to fuck the little blonde
Who brought around the fucking cherry pie!

Yesterday I passed a fucking site
Where three young workmen cursed their fucking luck;
One said he'd like to fuck old Fuck-face White;
They all agreed — "Lets fuck the fucking Fuck!"

THE SOCKDOLAGER

for Joshua

Bird-bedazzled boy,
just ten,
you have hit New England
with all the June joy
of an astrologer
meeting a new star.
So far,
because, perhaps, they match your head,
you find the scarlet tanager
and cardinal
most fabulously red.
With what outrageous
gaiety you guess
how the goldfinch would be a cinch
to catch, gently, in your hand's hot cage,
keeping him just long enough
to feed him sweets of candytuft
and watercress
and cool white saxifrage
until, gathering with Johnny-jump-up grace,
you'd loft him, bright dandelion,
towards some deep, green,
bug-delicious place.
You fling your somersaults
against the air, aware
that we might call you onager,
the family name for ass,
but lying, laughing, on the grass,
you only care that the lesser-yellow legs
is in the marsh;
deer drink; blue cohosh blooms;
and if the fox inhabits
lairs where he devours rabbits —

and if the loon does seem to grieve —
you like it:
it is serious and beautiful.
You still believe
the chewinks cheer the fallen leaves
with scufflings of warm apricot,
rustling, nestling,
whistling *drink-your-tea*.   .

You level your binoculars;
a redstart lights a tree.
Half-jocular, I ask you
what you want to be when you grow up.
Your glasses swerve,
two rapt and distant moons;
you say, "Oh, ornithologer."

Crimson chat, uncommon
loon, I name you
Red
        Sock-
              dolager.

An Answer

Up here
I brood, stare
as if long gazing
at the pond
might bring me
spare
transparent
answers

This morning
when I wake — look —
there
sailing into sight

one mother
and her trail —
eleven
baby
hooded
mergansers

Hortus Conclusus

We knew they were there,
heard behind pine, chokecherry, spruce,
saw tail flicks, wing flirts,
learned songs, seasons, habitats,
the cowbird's ruse:
we bought large, illustrated books,
Sibley, Peterson,
to study and compare
and strong binoculars,
each lens cross-haired,
then a feeder
full of tiny grains and seed.
As if for Orpheus,
birds leave swale and thicket,
to come and feed.
First, chickadees and purple finch,
then red-winged blackbirds hunting
for spillage in the grass,
two indigo bunting —
one a heart-stopping blue —
the chipping sparrow, warblers
new to our eye.
We do nothing but stare,
replenish black thistle
and sunflower seed,
name the cedar waxwing,
bobolink, dicksissel,
scarlet tanager, the yellow-throat.
You switch on the radio for weather —
a voice blares — bomb —
Oklahoma — Terre Haute —
Kin… death…
We lunge, we choke it off
to concentrate again on birds;
sparrow hawk, whip-poor-will,

thrasher, crossbill,
killdeer, shrike, the mourning dove.
We both are short of breath
but search our books for Latin names —
(*Progne subis, tyrannus tyrannus*)
a brand new set of words,
determined to regain it —
our paradise; our birds.

LINES FOR MY VIRTUAL HEADSTONE

Up in Grammie's sitting room,
snow falling, birds flocking to the feeder,
I discovered I could read.
Locked upright in her rocking chair,
Gram said to mother,
hurrying in from somewhere —
She's been still as a mouse for over an hour,
looking at her book.
Joan's like my birds — naturally good.
I fill with happiness
although Gram has not understood.

Ruth Buckalew,
told me in 1942
that she had been watching me
for years —
that I used to wear gillies and a red plaid coat
and that she knew
I was going to be a star
someday.
You are going to be a star.
I remember meeting her on Washington St.
a few weeks after her marriage.
I looked her up and down,
said — you don't show it.
She turned bright red;
What did you expect, fresh kid —
a scarlet A?
a baby carriage?

My cousin Ben, also in that banner year,
1942, said — I forget the occasion —
If I wasn't me, I'd want to be you.

My British English teacher,
Ethel Johnson, remarked one day,
You *have a very happy way of writing,*
don't let them change that at your college.
Then I used "canorous"
in a theme; she said the word did not exist.
She sent me to the library to look it up,
promised to write it on the board
five hundred times if I could prove her wrong.
I came back chanting
softly, *canorous from Latin* canor,
tune, melody; tuneful, like a song —
from Latin canere, *to sing.*
She began to write the word
in slanting lines. The chalk screeched,
the blackboard filled.
My classmates sent me Churchill's sign,
the V, behind her back;
finally, the bell rang, sweet gong —
I blurted out
how brave she was and bolted
down the hall,
hating words, girls, Latin,
myself most of all.

Kenneth Burke wrote,
at Bennington, his kindly praise —
words like "nourish" and "flourish"
were in it. I was thrilled but
this was the clincher:
her work on Joyce's Portrait
was especially fine;
I plan to nab two of her points
and pass them off as mine.

I fell for you, K., in part, because
you lived in Greenwich Village —

had that Putney brio;
sometimes witty, often slow;
handsome. You told me once
I love two things: you and the San Remo.

After Parents' Day at Killooleet,
Ethan told us that his cabin mates were wowed —
They think you're both terrific,
so really — uh — neat!
He blushed but kept on going —
You make me — uh — incredulously proud.

Tim Andrews directed me as Mme. Rosepettle
in *Oh Dad, Poor Dad.* I got a rash
from the distress.
I hated it, the part, the play.
He said keep at it; you'll get it,
you are an actress.

Doris Dodge — my smartest peer —
read my dissertation, told me —
In an earlier life, you were Shakespeare.
I had felt that too.
Not arrogance — just the uncanny finding
that his places, plots, I already knew.

Tim confessed just recently, although I always knew it,
you're the only woman I really wanted to sleep with,
then added, but Darling, isn't it lucky that we didn't do it?

I lay in bed; high fever and the flu.
The doorbell rang;
a dozen scarlet roses were pushed through.
The card read,
We love Shakespeare. Please get well.
We love the way you teach him too.
        Michael Strauss, Alex Kerr, Bob K.
Just wily students plumping for an A?

I blessed them, all three,
consumed with delight in my auto-da-fé.

After the workshop, Frank wrote
on a page of his new book, *Desire* —
words which I hope he meant
but deeply doubted,
honor — superb — astonishment;
but by far the best
was when he told us of his adoration
for the insurmountable Mae West.
I said I'd seen her once, in Boston,
in *Katharine Was Great.*
You saw her, in the flesh?
I might have been the Blessèd Virgin Mary
or Maria Callas. I thought that we might kiss —
You really saw Mae West?
Oh Joan, what unadulterated bliss!

I re-read these recollected lines, groan,
vow my ashes will be scattered under pine
and simple flowers of the field;
wild gentian; purple loosestrife.
No burial — no egocentric stone
commemorating promise unfulfilled.
I reproach myself as actress, poet, mother, wife;
then borrow James Wright's haunting line —

I have wasted my life —

say it, love it, but ruefully admit,
though true in some small part —
and canorous —
                        it is not mine.

V

THE POET'S WIFE IMAGINES

His wind-lashed eye scans the meadow
Back and forth, back and forth,
As if for larks, though long-since flown.
Soon, they startle and arise;
He spurs them into half-heard song
Then sings strange music of his own.

Inside, the coffee burns his tongue.
He swears but will not leave the larks.
He thinks of Shakespeare and of Shelley
Glad to have these poets near
But gladder still — this windy day —
His wife away, to be at work,
                    utterly alone.

Rabbits

You might have thought things would come right again
If you could only keep quite still and wait.

"Myxamatosis" Philip Larkin

Today, I saw a rabbit
down by the clump of wild blue flags,
nibbling grass, the sun, as if on silk,
gilding its long soft ears.
By what miracle do you survive
up here in this rough countryside
where four loved cats in alternate years
have been eaten alive? Tears
well up, fill my eyes.
The rabbit hops towards the iris,
disappears. I am bewildered,
excited by the presence of the rabbit,
what it prophesies.

The summer Aunt Bunny went mad
(if you called Uncle Phil
you could hear her scream nearby)
their rabbits got hit with myxamatosis.
I asked my mother if the rabbits
caught it from Bunny.
You are not one bit funny!, she snapped.
Later, I heard her chuckling
in the kitchen.
I loved to make my mother laugh.

Cherry Lane's father took us
to the races near Miami.
(We were there for mother's quick divorce.)
Greyhounds followed a mechanical hare
around and around the lit track.
I told Mr. Lane, This is so unfair,
the dogs can never catch the hare.

Lucky they're dumb, said Mr. Lane,
as he bet on Tommy Manville, Mr.
McGregor, Attila the Hun. We smiled
when they lost.
Cherry and I had no money but chose
the name Scheherazade. She seemed to scorn
the silly hare, a painted carrot in its mouth,
running just to run.
We went wild, jumped and screamed,
when, against all odds, she won.

When Bibi and I babysat Pat, who was four,
so the Wilcoxes could go to a faculty do,
we started to tease her. I said
When the donkey flies to Florida,
the leverets and conies pony up, keep score.
Ask your Daddy about the uxorious
William Blake, his sickrose wife.
Do bunnies like Blake? Cottontails cotton up.
And plankton too. Picasso's picture especially!
See Dali in a desert with a melted watch,
breeding lilacs, mixing memory and desire
as the cow rabbit-punches the big bad moon.
Bibi clucked and mooed, gave one high hop.
Pat started to shake, then cry.
We gave her chocolates and cambric tea
to calm her down, patted her furry bunny slippers.
Later, we laughed, told Annsy and Chat
how easy it was to drive a little kid mad like that,
stringing non-sequiturs up in a row.
They didn't smile, both pure ice. It took all
my charm and several days
to win them back. Like little Pat.

Les Duranthons, Robert et Cecile,
invited us to dinner, a first from the French.
Laundry was strung across the hall,
still dripping.

She had beads of sweat on her lip,
the usual stains under each arm.
After the excellent bouillabaisse
came a rabbit,
head attached,
eyes open, long lashes singed.
I felt faint,
pushed my slice around the plate,
found a small trench in the *haricots verts*
for camouflage.
Robert talked about the war, his long
internment.
He was captured near the Maginot Line.
I'll kill a German yet, he declared.
She asked me if I liked *lapin?*
I said yes but *je suis pleine,*
playing the dumb American.
They all laughed — freed.
I studied the wall, the arch of the door
but no matter where I looked
the rabbit's scorched eyes stared
straight into mine. As if on cue,
I began to bleed.

Mademoiselle Le Lièvre came to our flat
on the Rue de Chazelles for dinner.
She taught me in the *cinquième*
at the Alliance Française.
My themes were meant to dazzle her.
She was blond, had rose-colored skin, Sèvres,
set off by the blue of her eyes and silk shirt.
You were enchanted. I watched you flirt
in your show-off, schooled, Geneva French.
After brandy, you offered to drive her home.
I took the keys, said No, I'll do it.
Night-blind, terrified of Paris traffic,
I was suddenly brave as Joan of Arc.
But the kind, alert Giselle Le Lièvre

insisted on taking the metro.
We walked her there in a gentle rain,
came back to the Rue de Chazelles
via the unlit Parc Monceau.
J'ai levé un lièvre you said, smug.
Later on I looked it up; had to smile.
To start a hare means in French
To raise a burning issue,
To touch a sore spot.
I turned toward the wall in our lumpy bed —
cold as ice, and all night long — white hot.

Years later, in Zagora, at Morocco's edge,
hoping to sight the legendary blue men,
we were served rabbit again. You
and the boys ate it happily.
I asked the Danish waiter why he was
here in this forsaken desert town.
Relief from asthma, he said.
Are the rabbits local?
He put two fingers across his lips,
shook his head,
Here nothing can grow.
His sadness hangs on him, blue as a shirt.
I think of him caged in his little room,
flipping the pages of magazines,
coming into his handkerchief,
the moon staring down, its mad golden eye.
He cannot leave; but unlike the rabbit,
that's why he's here, to trust the air,
to breathe.

Tonight, when I dug up the Stevens poem,
"A Rabbit as King of the Ghosts,"
Yes in the margin,
I knew how much he was a rabbit,
why I felt so close to him,
how comfortable it was to hunch down

in the grass and simply wait for danger
to subside, no sign of cat or fox,
the cat now a bug in the grass, the grass
like a nest, his amenable hosts.
Nothing to trouble the rabbit light
or dog his importance, his calm —
except those anterior words: *Rabbit, Ghosts.*

for Matt Wallaert

A Visit To My Mother's Grave

I'm going to try to tell the truth
About my mother, Margaret, and Kendall's mother, Ruth,
And me. I'll try to edit out the sentimental
Or the very grave but I need this act of burial
Judged. You see, my mother wanted to be burned
To ash and scattered, "Returned
To Nature," as she grandly said,
"The one way for a Pantheist, deemed dead."
There is a hillside behind the house
She lived in where hepatica, ruffed grouse,
Bloodroot, wild violets flock in spring.
She loved these. She said her heart did, actually, sing
When, in winter, she imagined this Elysian scene.
This was where she wanted to be strewn.
But when she died, I took the box of ash
From Mr. Poole (I called it "sacred trash,"
He blanched) and brought it to our summer place
In Rochester, Vermont. "A disgrace!"
I hear you think. But wait! I'm alive, she's dead.
I need her near me until my head
Goes dark and empty too. I think about how moss will map
Her presence in her absence like a long lost lap.
Kendall, my sons and I dug a hole in our north field
And put the metal box inside, still sealed,
Unable to scatter her loosed ash,
Crying, mute, unpracticed at this task.
We placed a marble marker on the covered box,
Strewed the earth with daisy, dittany, wild phlox
And other blossoms near our gleaning hands.
Our weeping welcomed Margaret to these lands.

There is one unalterable truth:
Margaret disliked this farm and Kendall's mother, Ruth,
Who bought it, prized it, gave it to her son,
And who, when mother visited us here, would stun

Us all with rude remarks and ruthless slurs.
My mother laughed about it, yet such vitriol stirs
In the memory and burns. Still, here she lies
To satisfy a daughter's need for uncut ties.
Sometimes I think I'll dig her ashes up
And take them to her hillside in Connecticut.
Then I know I'll leave her here to lie,
Though discontented, until I'm boxed in near her when I die.
Does Ruth, in the lower meadow, under stones,
Know that Margaret's here, asking "Joan's
Mother? Mag? In my upper field?"
I 've crossed them both. They are "unhousell'd, unanel'd."

Will Christopher and Joshua and Ethan dare
To sow my ashes freely on the air?
Or will they joke about the clinkers they've untombed,
Those stubborn joints and bones not quite consumed
By fire? Is there an after-life? Do the dead have rights?
Does consciousness haunt their nights
And days? We're vexed because we cannot know,
But, like Prince Hamlet, wonder, brooding as we go.

I think of Bartie, ashes blessed by David in a graveyard rite,
Which, when scattered, whitened his black shoe, a sight
That shook me into laughter, though suppressed;
Bartie's bitchy lust for life artfully expressed.

I went to visit Margaret's stone again today
And took these dogged couplets up to say
Aloud. The goldenrod and Queen Anne's lace and dittany
Bloomed still. They nodded at my litany
As if they too were half-consoled by steady rhyme,
And certainties like loss and love and passing time.

September Noon

A mockingbird sits in the crabapple tree.
He returns my gaze, as if reflectively,
and why not? We are distantly related.
His unruffled stare takes me in, antiquated
shape in a white, wicker chair.
A summer nest, he might think; some woven lair?
As if to sing, he cocks his head,
then topples off the branch — plumb down — dead,
a thing that I have never seen before.
Birds usually hide their deaths; dark thicket, ferned floor.
Two bats fly from the barn as if crazed;
I think fugue — call out "John!" amazed
as my cat stops in the midst of his stalk-
ing, falls, turns, legs going as if to walk,
then stops. Dead too. An owl hits the ground
to my left, "whoo," his last cartoon-like sound.
The air smells sweet; is it plums? apricots?
Things spin; I hear two dizzy shots,
try to focus, rise, stand,
totter, blank out — sit down on my bad left hand,
hard, knowing now just how I'll die.
(The phone is ringing — some child's goodbye?)
Not by Frost's fire, not by his ice,
this toxic windstream will suffice.

I hear myself gurgle — a cow — mad — moos —
lungs burn — I gasp — need oxygen — breath —
ask who's left to broadcast inaudible news,
who to bomb Babylon back to dumb death?

The ghost of the mockingbird sits in the tree
mocking war, its boys, insanity.

March Simile

Like old cellos
                    found in a boarded-up house

by boys
                    who have never played a note

but are over-joyed
                    at finding these things

with the fat-lady shape

                    who take up rusty bows

of course
                    skreek them against the startled

strings

and scraw
                    and scrape and rasp and wheeze

until that discord
                    starts to sing

Messiahs
                    at their gospelling

the starlings
                    in these bare-limbed trees

The Underpass

Few get on at Fernwood
scruffy place — idyllic name;
then we stop, some whim of the local train
in an underpass dim as an ancient wood.

I see a dark thing: the beast with two backs,
a man, large, his exposed backside
thrusting and plunging, a bronco ride —
into a boy he has pinned by the tracks.

I can see the side of the boy's choked face
thrashed with tears of rage and pain,
the big man bucks and bucks in vain
hand whipping his mount in a tortuous race.

What can I do — scream, smash, crack
the glass, somehow save the battered boy?
The train pulls out from this sack of Troy —
transporting us home to our rape of Iraq.

Parce que

The French lady in the blue silk dress
jammed hard metal in my back,
marched me here, bound me to this post.
The rope is fat, twisted, a knot
at the end, the kind my father used
to punish his dogs.

Why?
Revenge? We've never met before.
My age and shape argue that it's not for sex.
Some kick she gets from others' degradation,
the need to hear the slurry and the slobbering of fear?

She smelled of sweat like Bernie and Annette
in Paris; it was nineteen fifty-four.
I knew just why they smelled like that —
because they were so brilliant and so poor.
Bernie later killed himself, no note,
no explanation.

Because was once my favorite word;
it joined two phrases like a bridge, a consolation.

After my father whipped a dog,
I'd crawl into the kennel late at night,
petting, stroking, crooning,
so the dog would know
we both were victims of injustice.
You have to pity him, I'd say,
because he is so weak, unhappy, mad.
It was nothing that you did.
Gun-shy Petunia licked my hand.
Did she remember? When she first shied,
then ran, he called her back,
took his gun and broke her rib.

I listen for the slur of silk —
no sound, no light.
I hope this is a dream, know I am awake.

One parallel I find: wrists aching, ankles nearly numb,
is with the world itself;
dark, unsparing, violent and dumb.

Near Les Baux

Forests
the excoriation of these trees —
By whom? Why?
The wind plays no music here
The raw wood weeps

Long ago, near Les Baux, in France,
we read the history of a man
écorché vif

Like deer among the skinned trees
I rise and lie down, nervous, alert

What the hell is wrong? he asks.
Smiling, I don an old pink silk sheath,
Remnant of our Paris days
Our new friends were trading husbands, wives —
Even in the upholstered Bois de Boulogne
I hated Paris and the French
            especially Danielle,
                    in her long, sutured, mink coat

Those lampshades are now clichés –
Like the shorn heads of French girls
Caught unbuttoning their Nazi boys –
German lampshades made of Jewish
Skin, we'd say, horrified, excited, young
Not yet convinced

Marsyas
He played the oboe made of wood and reed
Exquisitely —

Did the Muses watch as their favorite, Apollo,
Tied him to a tree
Lyre silent at his belt
Then flayed proud Marsyas alive?

They did

THAT BLUE REPAIR

Elizabeth Pierson Friend (1933-2003)

When I heard Elizabeth had died
I tried to ease the pain of grief and rage
by walking fast around the pond.
Beyond the grove of trees we call *the copse*,
I stopped — amazed — by myriad birds,
blue jays, finches, waxwings, crows,
warblers of some olive hue, mourning doves,
one bunting, heart-stop blue — all flying
in and out of bushes, maple, cherry, pine,
ruffling, chirping, fluttering as if in agitation.
I stood stock-still. Were they sharing berries,
seeds, just darting in among the leaves in sallies
and quick flirts for some salient reason?
Their wing-beats made a fretted music —
one I'd never heard before; fugue —
orchestrated flight?

My scored heart beat. Elizabeth, I felt,
was there, implicated in this sight.
Perhaps the colors of the paints she used
had taken on the form of birds
to celebrate her wit, her bravery, her vivid art —
composition without words.

Each day I quietly approach the grove,
thinking of Elizabeth, to see if any of her birds
are there. Unfairly — none.
Once, one swallow, out of season.
I think about the myth of Philomel —
how she wove the story she would tell
before the gods transformed her
to a nightingale. I let that go
then ask Tracy, who knows every bird, its song,
its habitat, for explanation. She is bewildered —

but remembers once, in Concord, on a winter walk,
about to visit Marnie who was close to death, seeing
bluebirds by the hundreds embroidering
the snow. Marnie smiled to hear of these, said
one moment of pure grace.

That congregation of ecstatic birds —
blue jay, goldfinch, bunting, dove —
was something real and rare, breath-taking
as sudden death, its wild despair.

I have no rituals of consolation
just these worked lines, their tearing out,
their weaving up, that blue repair —
a labor which may bring in time,
if no return,
amending love; resignation.

My thanks to the following friends, critics and teachers
who have given so generously of time and expertise:
Nathalie Anderson, Ann Aspell, Peg Boyers, Jessica Fisher,
Ben Foster, Jim Freeman, Sandra Kohler, Joshua Landis,
Jeanie Levitan, Jeanne Minahan McGinn, Anni McKay,
David Outerbridge, Luis Prado, Cynthia Ryan, Vijay Seshadri,
Joe Schenkman, Kathryn Schenkman, Elaine Terranova, Lesley Valdes,
Matthew Wallaert, Richard Wilbur, Tracy Winn,
And fellow poets of the New York State Summer Writers Institute,
With special gratitude to Frank Bidart.